More Lessons From Bible Characters

By

Michael Imhof

TEACH Services, Inc.
Brushton, New York

Scripture taken from the New American Standard Bible,
Copyright © 1960, 1962, 1963, 1968, 1971, 1972, 1973, 1975,
1977 by the Lockman Foundation. Used by permission.

Cover format by Jennifer Reese

Published by

TEACH Services, Inc.
WWW.TSIBooks.com

Contents

Dedicated to persecuted Christians throughout the world who persevere for the sake of the gospel.

Introduction

Based on the outstanding success of my first book on lessons from Bible characters, I decided to do a sequel. The format is very comparable to my first book on this subject. As a matter-of-fact, in some cases, the lessons are comparable to previous lessons I addressed; however, the situations are all different and some new characters are introduced into this sequel. I wouldn't write this sequel if I didn't believe it would be beneficial for the edification of one's spirit and soul. There are some key lessons for us all to receive in this little book.

Thirty-five situations are examined, and again, short summaries and simple conclusions are made for everyday living. Each section is presented in a simple and understandable way. I also decided to include sections on the seven churches in the Book of Revelation. Although these were churches in John's day, they actually represent churches for all generations. Even though these churches were geographically located in current day Western Turkey, their lessons remain valid for today's churches throughout the world. That's why all seven of them are included.

I pray this book will be a blessing for you. Some conclusions are strong but truth is important and needs to be confronted in order for us to make the proper adjustments. Maintain a good attitude and be receptive to what the Holy Spirit would have you to receive. I pray you'll be able to apply these simple lessons to your life.

1

The First Martyr

In today's world people selected for promotion have typically done a good job. In the Book of Acts Stephen was selected by the congregation, among others, to serve tables, i.e., tables of food for widows. Qualifications to serve were to have a good reputation, to be full of God's Spirit and to have wisdom. Stephen met those qualifications. Based on these qualifications and my own personal perceptions, I also believe he had a spirit of excellence and an attitude of servitude. These attributes often go with a good reputation.

It's easy to see that Stephen was a devout disciple, a diligent man. He quickly gained a reputation for vigorous evangelism as evidenced by scriptures from the Book of Acts. Signs and wonders followed him when he ministered among the people. His prominence developed to the point where he was recorded as the first martyr after preaching before Caiaphas and the Council in Jerusalem. Stephen's sermon before this group is the longest recorded in the Book of Acts. After focusing on the privileges of Israel and their rejection of God's messengers, he then lays the blame of Christ's death directly on the hearers. This led to Stephen being stoned to death. Even as he fell to his knees, he asked God to forgive them.

Several things can be said about Stephen. First, he had a good reputation, spirit of excellence and an attitude of servitude. This allowed him to be selected for increased responsibilities.

Second, he was full of God's Spirit and was wise. This indicates to me that he was a diligent disciple and doer of the Word, not hearer only. Signs and wonders followed his preaching.

Third, he was bold in the things of God. His sermon before Caiaphas and the Council unequivocally supports this. No compromise here for he was a man of conviction.

Fourth, he was compassionate and forgiving as evidenced by his last words before death. These actions remind us of Jesus shortly before he breathed his last breath on the cross.

In summation, Jesus, in honor to Stephen, stood to His feet to receive Stephen's spirit into His kingdom as the stoning was being completed. The attributes of Stephen are exemplary. His personal characteristics and walk with God beacon as a light for us all to emulate; thus, let us learn from this man of God.

2

At The Midnight Hour

Trials and tribulations occur in life. Anybody living knows this to be a fact. There will be many opportunities to worry in life. No one is immune from problems that occur in day-to-day living. Even so, God does not want us to worry. He's very clear about this throughout the Bible. I once heard from a minister that "fear not" appeared 365 times in the Bible. That kind of repetition tells me something.

This introductory paragraph leads me to Paul and Silas when they were in Philippi. The chief magistrates in the area had ordered that Paul and Silas be beaten with rods and thrown into prison. Their feet were fastened in stocks after having received many blows from the rods. Human nature told them that they had been mistreated and were in a real fix. Human nature cried out against a dismal situation, and that it was now time for them to worry on how they were going to survive. Just look at their situation and I think you'll agree. They had been beaten, ridiculed, and locked away in a dismal and dark prison. They were probably tired and hungry as their bodies ached with pain, and yet, although they had a wonderful opportunity to worry over their circumstances, they did not. At about midnight Paul and Silas were praying and singing hymns of praise to God. I don't believe they were praising God for their predicament but for their deliverance.

These men were dead to the world and its circumstances and were alive unto God and His deliverance. Their part was to petition God; His part was to bring the deliverance. I believe they were casting their cares on Him. (I Peter 5:7).

Their circumstances said that they were done for. Their trust in God said no way. Suddenly, as they were praying and praising God, a great earthquake came and the foundations of the prison were shaken. The prison doors swung open and their chains became unfastened. Subsequently, this led to the Philippian jailer and his family becoming saved and later victories for Paul and Silas in their lives.

It's important for us to remember that God is concerned about every area of our lives. He's concerned about every situation and won't let us down as we trust in Him. Troubles of one type or another come to all lives. When they come to yours, remember your deliverer. He's able and willing.

"The Lord is good, A stronghold in the day of trouble, And He knows those who take refuge in Him." (Nahum 1:7). "Though I walk in the midst of trouble, Thou wilt revive me; Thou wilt stretch forth Thy hand against the wrath of my enemies, And Thy right hand will save me." (Psalm 138:7). "Be anxious for nothing, but in everything by prayer and supplication with thanksgiving let your requests be known to God." (Philippians 4:6). "I will lift up my eyes to the mountains; From whence shall my help come? My help comes from the Lord, Who made heaven and earth." (Psalm 121:1–2). Trust in the Lord and His deliverance.

3

Use Your Talents

The story of the servants and talents in the Book of Matthew provides lessons indeed. The master has three slaves that he entrusts his possessions to before going on a journey. One servant receives five talents, one two talents, and the other one talent. The one with five talents traded and received five more talents. The one with two talents traded and received two more talents. The last servant buried his one talent in the ground. Now after a long period of time the master returned and settled accounts with them. The two with the ten and four talents were commended by the master; however, the one with the one talent who hid it in the ground was labeled a wicked and lazy slave. His talent was taken away from him and given to the one who had the ten talents.

I believe this is a contrast of those who use their abilities from God for His glory and of those who do not. God has given us all some measure of abilities. I believe God wants us to develop our abilities and do well where He has placed us. God has called us to different walks of life but with the same commission. Some have been called to be carpenters, plumbers, teachers, pastors, evange-lists, salesmen, secretaries, bankers, soldiers and so forth. Regard-less of life's vocation, all are called to shine their light, spread the gospel and serve in Christ's body.

God needs people in different walks of life to reach out to people in their areas of assignment so to speak. He needs people to be faithful, pray and further His kingdom with their talents and abilities. God tells us through the story of the three servants that it's important to be faithful to the Lord and to use our abilities in serving Him. God commends faithfulness but looks poorly on indolence and indifference.

The three servants later gave an account to the master. We, after this life, will give an account to the Lord. Were we faithful? Did we use our abilities to serve Him? Were we lazy and indifferent about the things of God? These are questions to ask ourselves now. We now have time to do something about these questions while the Master is still gone.

Accounts will be settled when we see Him face to face. Let's use our talents to the best of our abilities and serve Him with faithfulness. Let's ensure all areas of our lives shine as a witness for Him.

4

Pharisee And Publican

The Pharisee and Publican went into the temple to pray. The Pharisee boldly proclaims to God that he's thankful that he's not like other people: swindlers, unjust, adulterers, or even like the Publican. He proclaims that he fasts twice a week and that he pays his tithes. The Publican, standing some distance away, was beating his breast and crying out to God for mercy while humbling himself. These two individuals provide a stark contrast.

The Pharisee was probably correct in what he told God. Yet, he was self-righteous and viewed others with contempt. Pride emanated from his demeanor. On the other hand, the Publican truly humbled himself and acknowledged his dependence upon the mercy of God. No pretense here, but a sincere and repentive attitude. The Pharisee came in formality while the Publican came in sincerity. The Pharisee doesn't even acknowledge himself a sinner while the Publican does. A self-righteous attitude, based solely on merit and good works, falls severely short in the eyes of God. A humble and repentive attitude gets His attention.

I believe it's important to live as righteously as we can in this life but always remember that Christ is the propitiation for our sins. We do not come to God on some merit system. Our debt is not paid through good works. Do good but come humbly and in reverence. Humility is important and speaks much better of a person than self-righteous pride. It always has, and always will.

In summation, Jesus said of the Publican, "I tell you, this man went down to his house justified rather than the other; for everyone who exalts himself shall be humbled, but he who humbles himself shall be exalted." (Luke 18:14). Maintain a humble attitude and reverence towards God. Stay filled with thanksgiving.

5

A Teachable Spirit

Apollos arrived in Ephesus and began teaching on the Lord. He was a Jew, Alexandrian by birth, who taught with a fervent spirit. He spoke accurately and boldly on the things he knew of the Lord. His eloquence greatly assisted him but there were things still to be learned. He had been baptized with the baptism of John, but not baptized with the Holy Spirit.

Aquila and Priscilla, devout and mature Christians, heard him preach in the synagogue. They then privately took him aside to expound to him more perfectly the way of God. They recognized the abilities Apollos possessed and desired to assist him in his endeavors. First, Apollos, an intelligent young man, was receptive to instruction. He humbled himself, and thereby, improved his message. Young Christians can learn from more mature Christians if they're receptive in the Lord.

Second, Apollos did not rest in his current knowledge but desired to know more. Christians should always strive to grow in the knowledge and ways of God.

Third, Aquila and Priscilla did Apollos a good service by instructing him privately. No public embarrassment took place. Aquila and Priscilla clearly recognized Apollos to be an earnest preacher of great ability. Ultimately, Apollos departed Ephesus and did great things for God.

Christians never arrive. There are many things to be learned as we grow in God. "For now we see in a mirror dimly, but then face to face; now I know in part, but then I shall know fully just as I also have been fully known." (I Corinthians 13:12). Always maintain a teachable spirit and desire to learn and grow in God. No matter how long one has been in God, one can always still learn and grow even more.

6

To Know More

Nicodemus, a member of the Sanhedrin, came to Jesus by night. Nicodemus was an inquisitive, well-intentioned pharisee who desired to learn more from Jesus. He approached Him by night since the chief priests would have become enraged over this kind of meeting. The chief priests, already upset over the teaching of Jesus, would have been disgusted just over the thought of Nicodemus meeting Jesus like this. Meeting Jesus at night also enabled Nicodemus to get Jesus' full attention, away from the crowded and mixed voices of daytime activity. Nicodemus came in earnestness, and approached Jesus with respect. He desired to know about Jesus and the miracles He performed. He recognized divine inspiration and authority before his eyes. Nicodemus' heart cried out to know the truth and more of it.

Nicodemus, in spiritual matters, was truly lacking in knowledge. Although he admired the miracles of Jesus, he had a hard time understanding that there must be a new birth, or change of spiritual condition in order to please God. Jesus makes it clear that the spirit must change. Receptive to the words of Jesus, Nicodemus did not turn his back on Him even though he was having a hard time understanding the words spoken to him. There was a willingness to be taught. There was a hunger to know more.

Some may criticize Nicodemus and say he strictly met Jesus at night because he was ashamed to be seen with Him in public. Let it be known that later he publicly spoke out for Jesus and attended to His body after the crucifixion. Small seeds grow. I believe Jesus clearly ministered to Nicodemus that night. As he heard more of Christ's teaching, and saw more of His power in operation, those seeds were consistently being watered and truth began to grow in Nicodemus' heart. I believe Nicodemus' ears were thoroughly attentive anytime he had the opportunity to hear Christ speak. He wanted to know more.

This brings us to an interesting question in our lives. Do we want to know more? There's so much more to the gospel than just salvation. Do we want to know more? To know more should be a cry of our hearts throughout our lives. Zeal for the things of God must not cease or grow old. Stir up that desire and seek to know more. God favors a desirous heart.

7

Impure Motives

Paul was arrested in Jerusalem and brought to Caesarea to stand before Felix the governor. Ananias, the high priest, came down with some elders from Jerusalem, and along with the lawyer Tertullus, accused Paul before Felix. However, Felix postponed decision on the case after the initial hearing. He wanted to await the arrival of Lysias, the commander who sent Paul to Caesarea from Jerusalem. It appears he wanted to hear Lysias' comments.

A few days later, Felix arrived with his wife Drusilla, a Jewess. He then sent for Paul and heard him speak about faith in Jesus Christ. Paul's teaching frightened Felix so he sent him away. At the same time, Felix was hoping Paul would give him some money so he could gain his freedom. Felix proceeded to do this quite often in the next two years, still hoping Paul would give him money. At the end of this period, Felix was succeeded by Porcius Festus, and wishing to do the Jews a favor, he left Paul imprisoned. Apparently, Lysias never made it to Caesarea to discuss the case, or Felix used his reference to Lysias in the initial hearing as a reason to put the accusing Jews off.

Felix is an interesting study. He was corrupt as a governor. His seeking a bribe from Paul during a two year period corroborates this. Were truth and ethical values important? Apparently not in the life of Felix. It must be deduced that his corrupt behavior in this small matter extended to violation of ethics in larger matters of government. His actions further show irresponsibility and lack of concern for others. Just please the Jews and leave the case for Festus. Perhaps this was a politically correct move in the eyes of Felix. Paul was held for two years and Felix never reached a decision on his release. Leaders who lead in governmental or public positions with an attitude like Felix's have no business being in office. One perceives Felix served himself and not the best interests of the people. Corrupt and irresponsible politicians will stand before God, as will all mankind, and give an account of their leadership.

In reality, anyone in any leadership position should lead morally and in concern for the welfare of the people. Responsibility should be executed with a conscientious attitude of excellence and service. Reject corruption and indifference. Serve the people with the heart of God, even in the small details of affairs. "He who is faithful in a very little thing is faithful also in much; and he who is unrighteous in a very little thing is unrighteous also in much." (Luke 16:10). Little things mean a lot and all people count in the eyes of God.

8

Cornelius

The first Gentile brought into the church was Cornelius, a devout man that feared God. He was a centurion in Caesarea of what was called the Italian cohort. A centurion was a noncommissioned officer who was in command of 100 men.[1] His men must all have been native Romans or Italians. He kept reverence of God in his household and was very charitable to the people. He continually prayed to God. It was in this setting that an angel appeared to Cornelius and told him to send for Peter in Joppa. Joppa was part of current day Tel Aviv.

Cornelius sent a dispatch to Joppa as instructed. As the dispatch was on its way, Peter was experiencing a trance from the Lord. Peter was wondering over the vision when the dispatch arrived. The Holy Spirit told Peter to meet the men and accompany them. So Peter and some of the brethren accompanied the dispatch back to Caesarea the next day. They arrived and met with Cornelius and his relatives and close friends that he had called together.

It was unlawful for a Jew to associate with a foreigner or to visit him, but God had shown Peter in the trance that he should not call any man unholy or unclean. Peter delivered the gospel message. The Holy Spirit came upon the Gentiles present and they began speaking in tongues. Peter and the brethren that accompanied him were amazed that the gift of the Holy Spirit had been poured out upon these Gentiles. Peter then ordered them to be baptized in water.

The angel told Cornelius that his prayers and alms had ascended as a memorial before God. God took notice. Why would God pick Cornelius out to be the first Gentile brought into the church? In summary, he was a devout man to God; prayed continually; humble towards God; and gave generously. I believe it's no different today. God takes notice of a devout and fervent believer who gives generously. Cornelius is a man to emulate.

9

David And Mephibosheth

King Saul repeatedly pursued David in his efforts to kill him. Saul's motives were clear so David had to flee and hide in the wilderness and caves. Eventually, after a long period of time, Saul and his son Jonathan died while in battle and David became king. This serves as background for the study of David and Mephibosheth.

Mephibosheth was the crippled son of Jonathan. David began to ponder and wanted to show kindness towards the household of Saul due to a previous covenant he had made with Jonathan. Even though Saul despised David, David and Jonathan had become as close as brothers. David remembered Jonathan and sent for Jonathan's son Mephibosheth to show him kindness.

Mephibosheth approached King David with fear and respect. It was not unusual for kings in those days to eliminate descendants of adversaries. Remember Mephibosheth was the grandson of King Saul. Mephibosheth had great concern and rightly so. King David, however, quickly reassured Mephibosheth that he wanted to show him kindness. David proceeded to restore his property and provided for his physical needs. This was such a beautiful example of kindness, forgiveness, grace and mercy. It also portrays a man loyal to his covenant.

David was said to be a man after God's own heart. (I Samuel 13:14). His actions towards Mephibosheth were thoroughly consistent with the ways of the Father. David, while honoring his covenant, displayed several attributes of God in this situation.

"And be kind to one another, tender-hearted, forgiving each other, just as God in Christ also has forgiven you." (Ephesians 4:32). "For of His fullness we have all received, and grace upon grace." (John 1:16). "Blessed are the merciful, for they shall receive mercy." (Matthew 5:7).

Let us activate kindness, forgiveness, mercy and grace in our lives. It will favorably affect lives and speak well of ourselves. Some may not notice but God certainly will.

10

A Time As This

The story of Queen Esther shows the importance of her role in the history of the Israelites. King Ahasuerus, after becoming disgruntled with Queen Vashti, replaced her with Esther. Soon thereafter King Ahasuerus promoted Haman and gave him authority over all his princes. Haman then developed a plan to try and destroy the Jews living throughout the king's Persian Empire. Queen Esther, already in place, was the one that foiled that plan.

Haman, full of pride, became infuriated when Mordecai would not bow or pay homage to him. Upon finding out that Mordecai was a Jew, Haman devised an evil plot to try and kill all the Jews throughout the land. He skillfully got King Ahasuerus to send letters throughout the empire calling for annihilation of the Jews. Mordecai, Queen Esther's cousin who raised her, approached her about the plot. Queen Esther asked that Mordecai get the Jews in Susa to fast for her. Esther demonstrated her dependence upon God with this request. Esther decided that she would approach the king, even though it was not lawful for her to do so.

Through arrangement of a banquet for King Ahasuerus and Haman, Queen Esther skillfully exposed the devious plot of Haman as evil to her and her people. Haman was subsequently hanged on the gallows that he had prepared for Mordecai. As a result of these events, the Israelites were allowed to rise up and defeat their enemies.

I believe Esther and Mordecai were right where God wanted them during this time of impending peril to the Jews. They were born for such a time as this. Their actions saved a multitude of lives. For those in Christ, I equally believe, they are born for such a time as this. Esther and Mordecai realized the importance of their actions. Christians today must realize the importance of their actions. Each Christian living today has the capability to touch a multitude of lives for the kingdom of God. Christians are placed in different walks of life throughout the world. By shining their light, and doing God's work where they are placed, the world will forever be changed.

Christians today are born for this hour. They need to realize this and accomplish God's work where they are placed during this last days harvest. "You are the light of the world. A city set on a hill cannot be hidden." (Matthew 5:14). "Set your mind on the things above, not on the things that are on earth." (Colossians 3:2). You were born for a time as this. Go forth and shine your light.

11

Issue Of Time

David knew he had been called to be king; yet, here he was hiding in a cave while fleeing the pursuit of Saul who was trying to kill him. (Psalm 142). It appeared at times that his flight would never end. Surely David must have wondered when the transition would take place under these trying circumstances. In that regard, much on his state of mind during this period of his life can be perceived from reading in the Book of Psalms. It's noted that David laments over his persecution and predicament but consistently retains his confidence in the Lord for deliverance.

The issue of time must be dealt with in each person's life. Samuel had told David that he would be king. David hid this in his heart. Yet, years passed before David came to the throne. David even had to flee for his life from Saul and spend days in the desert and caves. He could have given up but continued to trust God. He had confidence that the manifestation would come. David refused to allow time to become his enemy. He encouraged himself in the Lord and trusted in God to bring things into place. His confidence was rewarded.

A person will often pray and believe in his heart for the answer. Then after a period of time he basically loses confidence in his request since the answer did not physically manifest. This is a disappointment to the person, and God, for God was still working it out on the person's behalf. Time can become an enemy if people aren't watchful about standing in faith. When this happens, it brings frustration and disappointment. Sometimes the physical manifestation may take place quickly and sometimes it may take a longer period of time.

David maintained his confidence and endured time. Despite the trying circumstances, David became king. "Let us hold fast the confession of our hope without wavering, for He who promised is faithful." (Hebrews 10:23). "Therefore, do not throw away your confidence, which has a great reward. For you have need of endurance, so that when you have done the will of God, you may receive what was promised." (Hebrews 10:35–36).

12

Capable Of More

Manoah and his wife received directions from the Lord that they would have a son. They were told the boy would be a Nazarite to God. A Nazarite was a layperson of either sex who was bound by a vow of consecration to God's service for a specific period of time or in some cases life. A Nazarite could drink no fruit of the vine, not cut his hair, and not defile himself by going near a dead person. These outward signs served as a public testimony of his dedication to God.[2] In the case of Manoah and his wife, the Nazarite vow would be lifelong for their son. The woman gave birth and they named him Samson.

Samson was blessed with great abilities and strength; yet, his life was filled with pitfalls. Early in his life he approached his parents about marrying a Philistine woman from Timnah. This was not typical procedure for an Israelite, especially a Nazarite, to marry a Philistine woman whose god was Dagon. His parents were not desirous of this marriage; however, God ultimately used it for his purposes. Thus, Samson went down to Timnah with his parents to arrange the marriage. A young lion attacked Samson along the way, and Samson with great might killed it.

The wedding feast provided Samson his first opportunity to stir up things with the Philistines. Thirty Philistine young men, provided by the wife's relations, kept Samson company while he conformed to the custom of celebration for seven days prior to the marriage. Samson, while entertaining his company, gives them a riddle to solve within seven days and places a wager on it. The men could not solve the riddle so under threat of burning the wife to be and her father's house, they get her to entice the answer of the riddle out of Samson. Samson proceeded to Ashkelon, killed thirty of their countrymen, and paid the wager with the spoils of his conquest upon return. Wager settled.

Samson returns to his wife to be, but finds that her father gave her to another in marriage. Samson immediately seeks revenge on the Philistines. He set their grain fields on fire by sending 300 foxes, broken off into couples, into their fields. Each couple had a stick of fire tied between their tails and ran terrified through the fields and vineyards. Much loss occurred, and the Philistines to get back at the wife's family, burned her and her father with fire. Ultimately, she perished in fire anyway.

This action against his wife to be and her father infuriated Samson. Samson then struck the Philistines ruthlessly with great slaughter in retaliation and fled to the natural fortress of Etam. The Philistines pursued and camped in Judah, looking for Samson. Then 3,000 men of Judah went to Samson to tell him that they were taking him to the Philistines. Samson tamely consented and was delivered to the Philistines in Lehi. The Philistines started to shout in victory but then Samson broke his bindings and used a jawbone of a donkey to kill 1,000 men.

The eventual fall of Samson occurs when he gets involved with Delilah after previously running with a harlot in Gaza. The Philistines wanted to know the source of Samson's great strength so they asked Delilah to find out and tell them and they would give her money. Samson eventually tells her that he's a Nazarite unto God and that his hair must not be cut. If it is cut, then he would lose his great strength. Delilah had Samson's hair cut while he slept and then delivered Samson up to the Philistines. They gouged his eyes out and brought him to Gaza in chains and placed him in prison.

Samson was now a source of amusement. He was reduced to slave grinding work, work normally performed by women. Then one day the lords of the Philistines assembled to offer a great sacrifice to Dagon. For folly, they called for Samson and had him placed between two pillars. The place was full of men and women, and all the lords of the Philistines were there. A great crowd participated in and watched the amusement. During his time since capture, Samson's hair had begun to grow back, and while he was standing between the pillars, he called on God for strength. He pushed the pillars and caused a collapse of support. The dead killed that day were more than those Samson had killed in all his previous days. Samson also died.

Samson, although endowed with great gifts, failed to fully use them for God's glory. He never fulfilled his great potential. Over the course of his life he got involved with paganistic Philistine women, and ultimately, it was a woman who led him astray and to his downfall. The pleasures of this world have led many astray. Ungodly decisions made in the temporal or spiritual realms have their rewards.

All men and women living in today's world have great potential. Potential is fulfilled when one uses their skills and abilities to bring glory to God and follow God's plan for one's life. Many are not fulfilling their potential. Let us not be one of them.

13

Try Again

Abraham had died and Isaac was now on his own. It was clear, however, that God was continuing to bless Isaac. His flocks and herds continued to increase and he became a very wealthy man. The Philistines living in the area, noting Isaac's prosperity, became envious of him and filled up the wells which were essential to Isaac's wealth. Subsequently, Isaac was asked to leave the area by the Philistines.

Isaac proceeded to the valley of Gerar. There he dug wells and found water. Unfortunately for Isaac, the herdsmen of Gerar argued about the water and claimed it as theirs. So Isaac proceeded to build another well, but the herdsmen of Gerar quarreled over it too. Isaac then moved away from there and dug a well in another area. Finally, there was no quarreling and success. Isaac endured the contention that was trying to clog the flow of God's blessing in his life and dug again. As he kept digging, the flow of God's blessings came forth again.

Perseverance is important to success. Disappointments come in life but one must not allow adversities and disappointments to stop them from pursuing their goals. Victory so often comes to those who persevere. They will not accept defeat but will try again until success is seized.

Thomas Edison was a man who persevered until he finally attained success. With vision in heart, he repeatedly persevered after numerous unsuccessful attempts until he invented the light bulb. Two quotes he made provide a bedrock of thought for everyday living. He stated, "There is no substitute for hard work" and that "genius is one percent inspiration and ninety-nine percent perspiration."[3] William E. Hickson agrees with Mr. Edison and reminds us, "Tis a lesson you should heed: Try, try, try again. If at first you don't succeed, Try, try, try again."[4] Be strong, persevere and seize victory.

14

A Valiant Warrior

Gideon was beating out wheat in the wine press when the angel of the Lord appeared to him. Times were tough under the oppression of the Midianites and Gideon was trying to thresh out what he could without it being seized from him. Gideon was stunned when the angel of the Lord called him a valiant warrior and told him to go and deliver Israel from the Midianites.

Gideon, well aware of the situation, cried out how he wasn't the man for the job. Even so, Gideon proceeded, at the Lord's direction, to pull down the altar of Baal and cut down the Asherah that was beside it. Gideon, through the Lord's help, was then able to gather men together to come against Midian. After the gathering of the men, Gideon used a fleece of wool to confirm the Lord was with him. God graciously confirmed to Gideon that He would deliver Israel through him.

Thirty-two thousand men now stood ready to go against Midian; however, the Lord told Gideon that it was too many. The Lord told Gideon that Israel would become too boastful and think it was solely their hands that gained the victory. Through a couple of tests, the number was narrowed down to 300 men. Then God said to Gideon that He would deliver Israel through these 300 men. The men took trumpets and empty pitchers with torches inside the pitchers as they approached the enemy's camp at night.

At the prescribed signal, the men blew the trumpets and broke their pitchers. They then held their torches in their left hands and blew the trumpets in their right hands. The smashing of the pitchers made great noise and allowed for sudden light to be seen. Fighting within the enemy's camp ensued among themselves and they fled for their lives. Fear immediately seized the enemy as they perceived a great army was being ushered in by trumpeters and torch-bearers. The power of imagination is impressive, especially when God's involved.

Gideon did not picture himself as God's deliverer. He perceived himself to be unfit for a service of this magnitude. Here again, God takes a humble man and encourages him to go forth in victory. Lacking confidence to accomplish this assignment, God confirms and reassures Gideon all along the way that He was with him to bring deliverance.

Today, even more so under the New Covenant, man is destined for victory as he follows God. Standing on the promises of God and being a doer of the Word will make any Christian a valiant warrior for the kingdom of God. Whatever the opposition or task, be humble minded but confident in victory. For those in Christ, God spells victory for He's with you. Take Him at His Word and blow the trumpet, smash the pitcher and lift the torch. Behold, victory awaits.

15

A Lesson From Adam

Adam and Eve were placed in the garden of Eden with instructions not to eat fruit of one particular tree, the tree of the knowledge of good and evil. The Bible records that Satan, through the serpent, tempted Eve to eat of this fruit. Eve ate and gave the fruit to Adam who ate willingly and knowingly. Sin now entered the world with all its consequences. The actions of Adam and Eve were more than just eating forbidden fruit. They placed their wills above God's will and disobeyed His word.

God confronted Adam on his disobedience and Adam responded by putting the blame on God for giving him Eve. He willingly took the fruit from Eve. Can you see this in our society today? Many in our society have not learned from this story. Many will not take responsibility for their actions. Many will blame others and use weak excuses for their wrongdoings. One will never mature in the things of God or in life until one is able to accept responsibility for one's actions. Adam refused to accept responsibility for his disobedience.

It's important for us to acknowledge when we do wrong and accept responsibility for those actions. Man must be able to confront and deal with his wrongdoings or his door towards rectification will remain closed. He may appear to escape consequences in some matters, but in reality, he doesn't. One must confront problems and not just glance over them. Deal with irresponsibility or its weeds will overtake your garden in life. "Now 'tis the spring, and weeds are shallow-rooted; suffer them now and they o'ergrow the garden."[5]

Be responsible for your actions. Realize when you've done wrong; confront your problem in truthfulness; and rectify towards a corrective solution. This approach to personal problems sets one on a path towards greater maturity in the things of God and life.

16

The Golden Calf

God called for Moses to come up on Mount Sinai to receive the Ten Commandments on stone tablets. Moses then went up to the mountain, and the cloud covered the mountain. The glory of the Lord rested on Mount Sinai and the cloud covered it for six days. On the seventh day God called for Moses from the midst of the cloud. Moses entered the cloud and was on the mountain for forty days and forty nights. The Israelites were getting anxious waiting for the return of Moses during this period so they approached Aaron about making a god.

Aaron, Moses' brother and assistant, gathered gold rings from the people. He used a graving tool to fashion a molten calf. The people rejoiced over the figure and Aaron built an altar before it. The next day the people rose early and brought peace offerings. The people celebrated as they sat down to eat and drink and then participated in some lewd debauchery.

The Lord told Moses of this developing corruption and directed him back to his people. Upon hearing of the situation, Moses interceded on behalf of his people for mercy. He reminds God that He had chosen Israel, that His name must be vindicated, and of the covenant He had made with Abraham. As God grieved, Moses returned to camp with the stone tablets to find things as God had told him. Moses' anger burned and he threw the tablets down and shattered them. He took the calf which they had made and burned it with fire. He then ground it to powder, and scattered it over the surface of the water and made the Israelites drink it. He confronted Aaron on why he would allow this. Aaron rationalized and blamed it on the people. The people were out of control so Moses stood at the gate of the camp and asked for people for the Lord to come to him. Order was restored as Moses ordered the execution of about 3,000 rebellious men. Moses then called for dedication to God.

Aaron had much blame in this situation. God clearly was not pleased with Aaron's leadership. He should have suppressed these events. God's anger against Aaron was not specifically recorded in the Book of Exodus of this incident, but it was later addressed in the Book of Deuteronomy. Fortunately for Aaron, Moses interceded for him, and Aaron was spared.

Two quick things immediately come out when looking at Moses and Aaron in this situation. First, Aaron was weak-willed and easily influenced by the crowd when he should have known better. His frivolous excuses were weak. Peer influence, not only affects children, but adults and leaders as well. Aaron refused to stand up for what was right but went along with the crowd. It's important to stand up for what's right, even in the face of majority dissent. A man of God will stand up for what's right.

Second, Moses interceded for Aaron and the people. His intercession saved many and proved the importance of intercession. Christians today need to intercede for others. Intercession changes things, and it's very apparent that this world seriously needs intercessors. Stand up for what's right and commit to intercession.

17

Winning Combination

Enoch is only discussed briefly in the Bible; however, it's very clear that he was a man of God. He was the son of Jared and of the seventh generation from Adam. He was the bright star of the patriarchal age and lived a long life before he was actually translated or taken to Heaven without dying. The longevity of the patriarchs (averaging 912 years, not including Enoch who did not die) may have been due to the canopy which was not dispersed until the Flood, or simply to the fact that it took some time for the effects of sin to shorten man's life span.[6] Genesis 1:7 seems to indicate that God suspended a vast body of water in vapor form over the earth, making a canopy that caused conditions on the earth to resemble those inside a greenhouse.[7] Regardless, during his years, Enoch developed a life of communion and fellowship with God.

The ungodly walk contrary to the ways of God but the godly follow His ways. I believe Enoch set God always before himself. I believe he consistently fellowshipped with God and followed His guidance. God's word was Enoch's priority and joy. Communion with God took precedence in his life over the carnal joys of the passing world.

I believe it was Enoch's daily business to seek the face of God and enjoy the sweet presence of God in his life. He bathed in God's love and sought it with an earnest and diligent heart. This was treasure in Enoch's life and he prized it greatly. He would not trade it for the things of the world. In reference to earthly affections, he was dead to the world and alive unto God. Enoch did not live like the rest. His glorious removal attests to the fact that he greatly pleased God. Enoch's heart was placed on the things that eternally and truly mattered.

Enoch lived a godly life but there's another side to his life's coin. It brings out something for us to be aware of. God delighted in Enoch's communion with Him. It's no different today. God delights in having communion with His people. He greatly desires it. He loves for His people to come to him and spend time in his presence.

It greatly pleases Him. I can't say this enough. To emulate Enoch will bring satisfaction to our lives and to the heart of our Heavenly Father. This is a winning combination.

18

Onesiphorus

My attention is keenly drawn to Onesiphorus, a Bible character in the New Testament. Paul mentions Onesiphorous in the II Timothy epistle. Onesiphorus served Paul in Ephesus and later searched Paul out in Rome and ministered to him while he was in a dungeon. Paul appreciated Onesiphorus and his faithful encouragement. Onesiphorus was strong in the Lord and Paul took note of his support.

One reason I single out Onesiphorous is that he's not a common figure in the Bible. There are Bible ministers in the world known by multitudes and then there are Christians in church pews known by relatively few. Onesiphorus, not as well known as Paul, Peter, John or others in Bible study, is still an exemplary example for us all to study. Little is written about him, but in those few words much is said. He was faithful, loving, giving, supportive and an encourager to others. Need an encouraging lift, listen to Onesiphorous. Need someone to help, Onesiphorous will be there. God thought enough of Onesiphorous to have his name recorded in the Bible.

God's work greatly extends beyond a sunday sermon. God has prayer warriors busy throughout the week. He has Christian folks involved in nursing home ministries or prison visitation programs. He has people passing out Bible tracts and working in rescue missions. He has multitudes involved in the ministry of helps and performing other good deeds. You may not know their names but God knows them.

You'll find people like Onesiphorous working among them. His attitude of servitude and noble traits should be found in all of us. "And when did we see You sick, or in prison, and come to You? And the King will answer and say to them, "Truly I say to you, to the extent that you did it to one of these brothers of Mine, even the least of them, you did it to Me." "(Matthew 25:39–40).

Love Is An Action Word

The story of the good Samaritan provides an interesting example of love in action. Jesus told the story of a certain man going down to Jericho from Jerusalem in the Book of Luke. The man fell among robbers; was beaten and stripped; and left for half dead. Both a priest and Levite passed this man in great need. Then came a Samaritan who demonstrated love and compassion by bandaging the man's wounds and bringing him to an innkeeper. He paid the innkeeper to help take care of the man. This was demonstrated love.

Much can be gained from this story. First, I think it interesting that Jesus tells of the Samaritan as being the good neighbor. The Samaritans were descendants of colonists whom the Assyrian kings planted in the area after the fall of the Northern Kingdom in 721 B.C. They were despised by the Jews because of their mixed Gentile blood and their different worship which was centered at Mount Gerizim.[8] Racism has no place in God's eyes.

Second, the Samaritan showed mercy and gave of his time and substance to help the beaten man, the others did not.

Third, he allowed his schedule to be interrupted to meet this pressing need. Perhaps the others considered themselves too busy to interrupt theirs. The actions of the Samaritan were clearly better than those of the priest and Levite and he was commended for them.

Many people today feign compassion for others in need by strictly speaking token words. Others overcome selfishness and demonstrate love through adjustment of schedules, giving of time and funds to help others in need. The story of the good Samaritan reinforces that love is an action word. People will take a can of oil to lubricate squeaky car doors, bicycle chains or rusty items. Once the oil is applied, those items work better. Love is a comparable lubricant in a needful world.

Henry Ward Beecher once said, "Of all earthly music that which reaches farthest into heaven is the beating of a truly loving heart."[9] I believe that statement finds favor with God. Love is part of God's character. "Beloved, let us love one another, for love is from God; and every one who loves is born of God and knows God. The one who does not love does not know God, for God is love." (I John 4:7–8). Love truly makes a difference in lives, for those in need of it and for those giving it. We're the better for it as we put love into action.

20

Rise Up

The Israelites were under the hand of Jabin, the King of Canaan, at the time of Deborah, a prophetess and judge of Israel. Sisera commanded Jabin's army and Israel was severely oppressed by them. Then one day Deborah sent for Barak and gave him directions from God that he was to march against Sisera at Mount Tabor after Deborah drew Sisera out. Barak agreed to go if Deborah also went. Then Deborah arose and went with Barak to Kedesh.

The scene shifts to Kedesh. Barak proceeds to gather 10,000 volunteers, chiefly from the tribes of Zebulun and Naphtali. It appears by Deborah's song that some volunteers had also come from other tribes. Word was sent to Sisera that Barak was on Mount Tabor. Sisera, confident in his 900 chariots of iron, proceeded to Mount Tabor with his powerful army. Deborah encouraged Barak to arise and go forth and defeat Sisera. Barak pursued and victory was gained. All of Sisera's army fell, not one of them lived through the battle. Judges 5:21 indicates the Lord sent a rain which flooded the stream and valley, neutralizing the chariots. A similar thing happened when Napoleon defeated the Turks in the same place in 1799 A.D.[10] Israel was delivered from the oppression.

In this story I want to focus on how Deborah and Barak rose up. Was there not a cause in the land? God clearly was involved in this victory but man had a part. It's no different today. God is looking for men and women to rise up and accomplish His will in the land. Deborah and Barak, after knowing God's will in this situation, rose up, and God gave the victory.

God's will for a land is laid out in the Bible. A land filled with righteousness where Jesus is Lord is His will. A land filled with drugs, murder, idolatry, pornography, homosexuality, and evil violence is not His will. No games here, just straight talk. God needs people to rise up today and pray in intercession. He needs people to set their desires on the things of God and commit themselves to his work. He needs people to rise up in spirit and leave apathy behind.

Prayer, repentance and commitment to the things of God, coupled with God's help, brings change to a land.

Is there not a cause? God says there is. "And My people who are called by My name humble themselves and pray, and seek My face and turn from their wicked ways, then I will hear from heaven, will forgive their sin, and will heal their land." (II Chronicles 7:14). Deborah and Barak rose up and saw victory in their land. Will we rise up and see victory in ours?

I think there's another item that can be added to the aforementioned as responsible Christians rise up. Christians need to intelligently execute their right to vote. Voting is a privilege in our land. It must not be taken for granted and it's an important tool available for use. Know the issues and who you are voting for and what they stand for. Your votes are important and they count. Vote wisely. It's part of being a wise steward.

21

Thomas

Jesus appeared to the disciples after the resurrection; however, Thomas was missing during the visitation. The disciples proclaimed to Thomas that they had seen the Lord. Thomas clearly understood their testimony but stated that he would not believe unless he saw the imprint of the nails on Jesus' hands and put his hand into the Lord's side. After eight days had passed, Jesus visited the disciples again. This time Thomas was present with them. Jesus spoke directly to Thomas and told him to touch his wounds. Thomas answered and said to him, "My Lord and my God!" (John 20:28).

Believing is a choice of one's will and not feelings. Thomas chose to disbelieve when initially confronted about the Lord's visitation. Jesus basically told Thomas to change his way about believing. Thomas saw, and now, he believes. Jesus went further to commend those who do not see but choose to believe. Once again, I state emphatically, believing is a choice. It's an act of one's will.

We see the process of choice in salvation when one accepts Jesus as Lord but what about the other promises of God? The other promises of God, which are plentiful, are also a matter of choice. Christians choose to believe, or not to believe, and act on them. It's an act of one's will. Feelings are not key to believing from the heart. As a matter-of-fact, feelings will often interfere for they're easily affected by temporal circumstances. Thomas provides a superb example of all the aforementioned.

A key lesson for us to gain from this is to take the promises of God and choose to believe them in our hearts. Act on them in accordance with God's biblical direction. Seeing before believing is not God's standard. Ask Thomas, he'll tell you. Believe first, act on His Word, and then the promise becomes reality.

22

Sin Blinds

Lot was sitting at the gate of Sodom when two angels visited him one evening. Lot proceeded to invite them into his house so they could spend the night. The angels initially declined but then accompanied Lot due to Lot's strong urging. He knew the danger they would face if they remained outside all night. Sodom was filled with riotous and debaucherous living. Homosexuality was common practice. Lot then prepared a feast for them and they ate.

Shortly thereafter, the men of Sodom surrounded Lot's house and began to yell for Lot's visitors to come out for they desired to have homosexual relations with them. Lot went to the doorway and pleaded with the men of Sodom not to act wickedly. He even tried to offer his two virgin daughters to the men of Sodom if they would not harm the visitors. Lot, through a custom of his society, was obligated to protect his guests.[11] Although this was not justified towards his daughters, it is explained in regards to the customs of his area and time. The men refused and persisted against Lot and tried to break the door down. The angels at this point pulled Lot away from harm and struck the men at the doorway with blindness. The men, in spite of the blindness, still tried to grope and come through the door.

These men of Sodom were given to homosexual behavior. It had become such a lustful part of them, that even after being stricken with blindness, they still tried to get to the angels staying with Lot. I believe this shows the depravity of these men and how sin blinds. It had such a grip on them that it appears to drive their wickedness beyond common reason. Demonic influence in these men was strong to say the least. Sin can become so entrenched in the lives of people that it can control their lives. Repeated practices of sin will create habits and eventually strongholds hard to break. Sin is not to be taken lightly or played with. Sin blinds and a blind man easily becomes lost. As one makes a mistake, one should confess, repent and get right with God. (I John 1:9).

Don't ignore and allow sin to become a practice. The words of Richard Chenevix Trench come to mind, "Sin may be clasped so close we cannot see its face."[12] I further add that once its face is recognized that it can become exceptionally hard to escape in many cases without the divine touch of God to set that person free. Sin will certainly work against you and not for your good. Thomas DeWitt Talmage sums it up, "Sin may open bright as the morning, but it will end dark as night."[13] Don't play with sin.

23

Hook Up

Paul's spirit stirred while he was in Athens waiting for Silas and Timothy to join him. He saw many idols in Athens that disturbed him. It was in the presence of these idols that Paul proclaimed the gospel to Epicurean and Stoic philosophers. Epicurean philosophers were followers of Epicurus (341–270 B.C.) who believed that happiness was the chief end of life.[14] Stoic philosophers, on the other hand, regarded Zeno (340–265 B.C.) as their founder. These followers emphasized the rational over the emotional and were pantheistic or allowed worship of all gods. Their ethics were characterized by moral earnestness and a high sense of duty, advocating conduct "according to nature."[15]

In the midst of these false beliefs, Paul was led by these philosophers to the Areopagus to share his ideas. Paul needed something to "hook up" with these people on in order to better establish rapport with them. He had noticed, among many idols, an altar with the inscription, "TO AN UNKNOWN GOD". Thus, he skillfully uses this as a lead in to the true God and the gospel. He proclaimed they need not be ignorant of this "UNKNOWN GOD" anymore. He had to gain their interest and relate to them in a manner where he would have their attention. Although some men sneered, some men believed in Paul's message.

The key point in this situation is that Paul found an area where he could "hook up" with his audience of unbelievers. As a result, some became believers. Christians need to learn from this story and apply this lesson when they're sharing the gospel with others. Managers and salesmen regularly practice it. Find an interest of your audience that you can relate to them on. People typically enjoy talking about their interests. Once the rapport is established, as the Holy Spirit leads, the gospel can be more effectively shared.

Interests of people are extensive. They include: sports; computers; travel; history; gardening; automobiles; cooking; and so forth. Some wisdom goes a long way. And He said to them, "Go into all the world and preach the gospel to all creation." (Mark 16:15). The commission still stands. Hook up and be led by the Holy Spirit. Paul hooked up, and as a result, some believed.

24

Demetrius

Paul was ministering in Ephesus on his third missionary journey. He was preaching and teaching with great results. Extraordinary miracles were taking place. Then there arose a silversmith by the name of Demetrius that opposed him and stirred up the workmen of similar trades. Silver shrines that Demetrius made of Artemis were not in great demand. Great profit was not coming in as people were being converted to the gospel truth. The idol business was being threatened. As a result, confusion was generated in the city as Demetrius appealed to the civic pride of the Ephesians by stating that the great goddess Artemis was being treated shamefully and dethroned from worship.

A magnificent structure built to Artemis was located in Ephesus and for years had been held in great esteem. So a great disturbance occurred in the city with many crying out for Artemis in protest of the recent teachings of the gospel. A mob mentality ensues as a result of Demetrius' actions. Truth is clamoured out by noise and misguided reasoning. Eventually, the town clerk under the providence of God, quieted and dismissed the crowd before harm was done.

Demetrius portrays a great zeal for Artemis but his true motive towards the conversions taking place was a loss of profit. Demetrius had great concern over the ways he obtained his wealth and set his efforts against the gospel of Christ. Is it any different today? Man must make a living, but when his trade directly opposes the truth of the gospel, it's time to change. Truth that has eternal consequences is more important. The gospel is not a game; it's an unequivocal reality. No man can effectually alter the commitment and weight of its truth.

The gospel truth is to be valued more highly than an unrighteous trade. I believe God will help a man who comes to the gospel out of an unrighteous trade into a new endeavor. God knows people have needs and He will help sincere hearts in their daily living to support themselves. To live a lie in an unrighteous trade and oppose the gospel is foolery. "For what is a man profited if he gains the whole world, and loses or forfeits himself?" (Luke 9:25).

Don't live a lie and sell your soul because unrighteous mammon is more important than a present and everlasting relationship with the Lord Jesus Christ. Unequivocally, Jesus is more important.

25

Don't Look Back

The setting of this section takes us to Sodom and Gomorrah. Two angels were sent by God to direct Lot and his family to leave Sodom and Gomorrah because it was about to be destroyed. It was a city well known for wickedness and sexual perversion and disaster was imminent. Lot and his family (wife and two daughters) initially hesitated, but with the assistance of the angels, were led away. Brimstone and fire then rained upon the cities. Deposits of sulfur and asphalt have been found in the area since. Possibly an earthquake occurred and lightning ignited the gases that were released, causing a rain of fire and smoke.[16] Lot's wife, who was trailing behind him, looked back and died. It appears that her heart was still in Sodom. The Bible says she became a pillar of salt. Perhaps she was enveloped by blowing salt which encased her body. Regardless, there's a serious lesson here.

Lot and his family had been instructed by one of the angels not to look back. Thus, Lot's wife disobeyed a direct command. She longed for her house and belongings. She desired to go back. Jesus later used Lot's wife as a warning for us all. Apostasy is to be shunned once we commit to Christ. We have renounced the world and the flesh and it's to our peril if we return to them. Apostasy is dangerous ground. Always press forward in Christ. Never look back.

The following scriptures provide clear warning about not turning back to the ways of the world and flesh after one is saved. "But Jesus said to him, "No one, after putting his hand to the plow and looking back, is fit for the kingdom of God." "(Luke 9:62). "For in the case of those who have once been enlightened and have tasted of the heavenly gift and have been made partakers of the Holy Spirit, and tasted the good word of God and the powers of the age to come, and then have fallen away, it is impossible to renew them again to repentance, since they again crucify to themselves the Son of God, and put Him to open shame." (Hebrews 6:4–6). These are strong words but important ones. Don't take them lightly.

Most assuredly, the best course is to maintain determined endurance and perseverance to the end. Don't turn your back on God and return to the world. God will reward you for your faithful diligence. Press forward in Christ.

26

Church Of Ephesus

The message sent to the Church of Ephesus is of benefit today. Christ knew their works and commends their diligence, perseverance and zeal against evil; however, there is a rebuke in his message. He states that they have lost their first love. The fervency for the Lord wasn't as it first was. More than 30 years before the Church of Ephesus had been commended for its love but now love is a subject of rebuke. Although diligent in works, their affections for the Lord had declined. Christ counsels them to remember their former state and revive that love within them.

There's usually a lively and warm affection for the Lord when one is first saved. This affection will eventually wane if time is not spent cultivating the relationship. It's a daily walk and effort is required to maintain that closeness. If time and effort are not spent in cultivating and maintaining the relationship, then affection will naturally slide. This is common in human relationships. Friends may grow up together and then move away. They remain friends but let contact go. Typically, the result is they're not as close as they once were. Time and effort are required on a consistent basis to maintain a close and fervent relationship with the Lord. It's a lifelong endeavor.

I think an example might be in order to further help get us on track. Take a golfer who doesn't play for quite awhile. Let's say his interest starts to slip or business has precluded his play, and he gradually doesn't think about it very much. Then one day a friend invites him to go golfing, so he goes. Then he goes again the next day. Pretty soon that fervency rekindles and his affection for golf is back. The lesson in this is to start spending quality time with the Lord. Rekindle that wonderful love you had for Him when you were first saved. Make your relationship with the Lord the priority in your life. It's worth it. He's a wonderful Lord who loves you very much.

27

Church Of Smyrna

People today can learn from the message sent to the Church of Smyrna. Jesus said He was aware of everything about their situation. Tribulation had come to these people. Many were outwardly poor; yet, Christ called them rich. He also knew of wicked ones among them. These wicked ones pretended to be covenant people of God when indeed they were inspired of Satan. He tells them tribulation is coming from Satan but not to fear. He told them to remain faithful and God would reward them.

Many lessons are presented in just a few verses of scripture concerning the Church of Smyrna. First, Jesus knew all about them as He knows all about us. He spoke to them with care as He speaks to us with care.

Second, many were outwardly poor, yet Christ calls them rich. I believe many were doing good works for the Lord and were solid in their attitudes towards God and fellow man. Many were rich in spirit; however, I don't believe the poverty was God's will. There are too many scriptures in the Bible that tell me God desires us all to live prosperous lives. I believe taking God at His Word, standing on His promises in faith, and being a doer of the Word will bring people out of poverty. "And let them say continually, The Lord be magnified, Who delights in the prosperity of his servant." (Psalm 35:27). "For you know the grace of our Lord Jesus Christ, that though He was rich, yet for your sake He became poor, that you through His poverty might become rich." (II Corinthians 8:9). "Beloved, I pray that in all respects you may prosper and be in good health, just as your soul prospers." (III John 1:2). "The Lord is my Shepherd, I shall not want." (Psalm 23:1). Yes, God wants us to be rich spiritually, but He also wants us to be prosperous. He doesn't want His children worrying about food or clothes. He wants to bless us in all areas of our lives.

Third, there were wicked ones among them. There are wicked ones among us today and God knows who they are. They may try and fool man but they won't fool God. "Therefore just as the tares are gathered up and burned with fire, so shall it be at the end of the age." (Matthew 13:40).

Fourth, notice who brought the oppression and tribulation. It was Satan, not God. Many peoplc today falsely accuse God of oppressive conditions and circumstances in their lives. It's not from God. "The thief comes only to steal, and kill, and destroy; I came that they might have life, and have it abundantly." (John 10:10). "Be of sober spirit, be on the alert. Your adversary, the devil, prowls about like a roaring lion, seeking someone to devour." (I Peter 5:8). Scripture tells us to resist the devil and execute our authority over him. "Behold, I have given you authority to tread upon serpents and scorpions, and over all the power of the enemy, and nothing shall injure you." (Luke 10:19). Many people are easy prey for the devil because they don't resist him and execute their authority over him.

Fifth, He tells His people to remain faithful and He will reward them. No matter what happens in this world, there's a great reward for those in Christ in the afterlife. Unequivocally, it's worth living for God. Nothing this world has to offer can substitute for God's eternal rewards. Press on.

Church Of Pergamum

The Church of Pergamum was situated in an area where much paganistic and idolatrous worship took place. Though many believed, there was still much corruption in the church. Some had gone the way of Balaam. Balaam, a figure in the Old Testament, hired himself out as a prophet and displayed deceit and covetousness in doing so. It is perceived that some in this church were displaying covetousness by loving wealth and prestige more than Bible truths. Some may have been doing religious works for personal gain. It should be noted that stinginess and self-righteous behavior often accompany greed.

Others in the church held to the teaching of the Nicolaitans. The Nicolaitans were followers of Nicolas according to the early church fathers. These were apparently a sect which advocated license in matters of Christian conduct, including free love, though some understand from the meaning of the name that they were a group which promoted a clerical hierarchy.[17] Regardless, this situation was not pleasing to God. Christ commends the church for their steadfastness but reproves them for their sinful failures.

Filthiness in the spirit and flesh must be dealt with. There was an ancient custom of giving a white stone to those acquitted on trial and a black stone to those condemned. To him who overcomes, Christ will give a white stone. Christ uses this illustration after calling them to repentance.

Much is said to the Church of Pergamum. The people involved in the corruption drew Christ's attention on the church as a whole. I think it important that a modern day church deal with corruption within its fold. To allow rampant sin to go on within its congregation is to play with fire. It will affect unity and prove displeasing to God.

It further should be noted that people serving God for personal gain do not escape the eyes of God. If one is in it just for the money, better reevaluate attitudes and priorities. A covetous heart is not pleasing to God. As God called this church to repentance, He calls us to repentance. He's quick to forgive as we come to Him. He has a white stone for us if we're willing to take it.

Church Of Thyatira

The Son of God, Who has eyes like a flame of fire, spoke to the Church of Thyatira. I believe reference to His eyes in this manner reflects his piercing insight into the affairs of man. Notice, as in messages to the previous churches in the Book of Revelation, Christ knows their deeds. He acknowledges their growth in love, faith, service and perseverance, but comes harshly against their toleration of wicked seducers that He compared to Jezebel. These wicked seducers attempted to draw the believers into fornication, and to offer sacrifices to idols. The patience of God was tested in that He allowed time for repentance but they repented not.

It appears these wicked seducers, led by a false prophetess, profess their teachings to be profound mysteries, but Christ calls these false doctrines teachings of Satan. Christ is tender towards His faithful followers but calls attention to the ones who need correction. Again, we hear the call of repentance.

There are many seducers of believers at work in the world today. There are false prophets, psychics, astrologers, and others in the world professing doctrines contrary to the true gospel. They may profess profound mysteries but God still calls them teachings of Satan. The gospel stands by itself without false doctrines being mixed in. Don't be fooled. If the teaching opposes biblical teaching, shun it.

Always compare what one says with the Bible. Does it coincide with biblical scriptures or does it violate them? Stick with the Bible. I say it again, stick with the Bible and its guidance. Don't mix false doctrines into your Christian faith. Jesus warned the Church of Thyatira then, and He warns us now not to do it. Let us heed His warning. It's for our own good.

30

Church Of Sardis

Christ addresses hypocrisy in the Church of Sardis. It apparently had a fine name and reputation and everything appeared well to an observing eye. However, in God's eyes this church fell short. There was a form of godliness but not the power of God at work in it. It was a dead church. There was little life left in it. He commands them to wake up out of their slumber. Don't just go through motions of religion but get alive unto God. Become watchful and strengthen yourselves in the things of God. God's alive and His church should be alive. He commends a small remnant who were walking with Him and considers them precious, but to many others, it was a stirring rebuke towards repentance.

There are many dead churches throughout the world. This message applies to them as well. Jesus is alive and He wants His people to be alive in the things of God. Jesus didn't stay in the tomb. Jesus raised from the dead and sent the Holy Spirit Who is at work in the world today, and He'll work where He's invited and allowed to do so. God wants His people to grow in Him. Based on that, if one is in a dead church and not being spiritually fed, then find one that's alive unto God. God cares too much for His people than to see them languish in a dead church. The building may look fine at a dead church, but in reality, it's not the church. The church is the people that attend it.

Once again, God is alive and He wants His people to be alive unto Him. He wants to surround them with His love and commune with them. He wants to bless them. He wants to show Himself strong in the concerns of their lives. He's a good God and he wants His people to know Him personally in an intimate way.

If you've been living a form of godliness and just going through the motions, then God is saying to you to wake up. He has more for you and wants to do more in your life. He who has an ear, let Him hear what the Holy Spirit has to say.

31

Church Of Philadelphia

The Lord commends the Church of Philadelphia. He says He has put an open door before them which no one can shut. I believe there was an open heaven over this church and it was alive unto God. I believe the people were edified during their services and that the Holy Spirit was present to minister to the needs of the people. I believe these people loved God and wanted to serve Him and do the work of the gospel. This church had its adversaries but they would not succeed against it for God was strong on their behalf. There were reasons for this. The people must have kept God's Word and were doers of it. Favorable results followed.

Revelation 3:10 indicates that this church would be kept from the hour of testing which was about to come on the earth. Many theologians believe that this is a promise that believers will be delivered from the tribulation period which will come on the entire earth. If this is so, then I take note that this promise was given to this particular church, i.e., certain type of believers. This is food for thought and I would be interested to find out what this church was doing right as well as to fellowship at one like it. "Then we who are alive and remain shall be caught up together with them in the clouds to meet the Lord in the air, and thus we shall always be with the Lord." (I Thessalonians 4:17). This event is commonly referred to as the rapture or blessed hope of the church.

There are many accolades in this message to the Church of Philadelphia. Obviously, the Lord is pleased with this church. The same is true today. I'm sure there are churches that please Him and there are churches that don't please Him. It's clear these people were alive unto God. Their lives showed it and God took notice. It matters where one goes to church. This message becomes clearer and clearer to me as I read all the messages to the churches in the Book of Revelation.

Christ encourages this church to hold fast to what it has. That means it could be lost if one is not watchful. A lazy man will not do well in the things of God. Believers are to be diligent in the things of God and vigilant against influences that detract from their walks. Christianity is a lifestyle.

32

Church Of Laodicea

Jesus has strong words for the Church of Laodicea. He immediately reproves them for being lukewarm. They weren't hot for Christ and they weren't cold for Christ. They were apathetic and comfortable in their wealth and sense of well being. There is no room of neutrality with Christ. He either wants you for Him, or against Him, not in between. Lukewarmness doesn't set well with Christ.

Laodicea was a wealthy city under Roman rule and it appears the Church of Laodicea was under self-delusion. Their physical man was well provided for, and in so doing, the necessities of their souls were being overlooked. Their spiritual man was starving in the midst of their abundance. They had high thoughts of themselves but Jesus saw them as poor towards God. They had slipped and become blind to the things of God. Christ counsels them to buy eyesalve so that they may see their condition. Laodicea was a center for making medicines, including a tablet that was powdered, mixed with water, and smeared on the eyes.[18] Perhaps this is why Christ used the eyesalve example to point out their blindness. Christ then encourages them to repent and to become zealous for Him.

Webster's New World Dictionary of the American Language defines zealous as, "full of, characterized by, or showing zeal; fervent; enthusiastic."[19] Jesus makes this message as plain as can be. He wants Christians to be zealous or fervent for Him. If a Christian is not zealous or fervent, then he needs to examine his walk with the Lord. There is no mistaking the Lord in His message to the Church of Laodicea. He wants us to be fervent. He's alive and we need to be alive unto Him. His counsel is to inspire us to fresh vigor.

There should be no room for indifference or lethargic behavior towards the things of God for his followers. It's important for us to receive His counsel and move forward with it. As we do, our lives will be more pleasing to the Lord. Any counsel of God is always to our benefit. Lesson to be learned—get fervent in the things of God. Stoke the fire.

33

Safe And Secure

King Belshazzar thought he was protected within the fortified walls of Babylon. He was holding a feast for a thousand of his nobles and gave orders to bring the gold and silver vessels which Nebuchadnezzar had taken out of the temple in Jerusalem during the 586 B.C. time period. The king, nobles, wives, and concubines drank wine freely from the vessels and praised the gods of gold and silver, of bronze, iron, wood and stone while doing so. The Medes and Persian armies were laying seige to Babylon but no need to worry. This was Babylon and Belshazzar was safe within its walls.

Ancient historians said that its wall was 60 miles around, 15 miles on each side, 300 feet high, 80 feet thick, extending 35 feet below the ground so that enemies could not tunnel under; built of brick 1 foot square and 3 or 4 inches thick; ¼ mile of clear space between the city and the wall all the way around; the wall protected by wide and deep moats (canals) filled with water; 250 towers on the wall, guard rooms for soldiers; 100 gates of brass.[20] One would say this place was well protected.

Suddenly, the fingers of a man's hand emerged and began writing on the wall before Belshazzar's eyes. The king's face grew pale and he called for the wise men to translate the inscription but they could not. So Daniel was sent for to translate the inscription. Daniel translated the inscription and basically told Belshazzar that God has given his kingdom over to the Medes and Persians. Belshazzar was slain that night and the Medes and Persians took control of Babylon. Babylon fell in accordance with Bible prophecies.

Many people in the world are living lives not pleasing to God. Many believe they are safe and secure in their own minds. No need to worry, time to enjoy life. After all, you only go around once in life. Different sources help generate this false sense of security. Perhaps it's wealth, a good job, or an indifferent attitude towards life. Whatever it is, one must evaluate their lifestyle in light of the gospel. Belshazzar, a wealthy king, thought he was secure; he was not. He lived a life of extravagance and pride and exalted himself against the Lord.

Many today exalt themselves against the Lord through bold defiance, indifferent living, or perhaps just a lack of desire to serve or know Him. No man is safe and secure from the judgment of God. A prize fight has 12 rounds. At the end of the twelfth round the bell rings and the decision is rendered. Don't be lulled into a false sense of security or your bell may ring. Safety and security are only found in God.

34

A Choice To Make

This section centers on a rich man and a poor man named Lazarus in the Book of Luke. The rich man lived his life in splendor and gaiety while Lazarus lived a poor man's life. The two died. Lazarus went to Abraham's bosom, a figurative speech for Paradise or presence of God, and the rich man went to Hades, the abode in this case for the unsaved. The rich man wanted to come back to warn his brothers for he was in great torment while Lazarus was in great comfort. The rich man was not allowed to do so.

Several points can quickly be gained from analysis of this situation. You'll notice the rich man retained his memory. There is a conscious existence after death. There are two distinct locations for abode, the reality of a wonderful paradise and the reality of a tormenting hell. There is no promised second chance after death to return as evidenced in the denial of the rich man's request to return and warn his brothers. The lives of the rich man and Lazarus were different during their earthly years and were most certainly different in their eternal destinies. The latter by far bears much greater importance.

What key lessons can be gained from the rich man and Lazarus in this story? First, realize there's life after death. Second, live your life in light of the eternal. There is a heaven to gain and a hell to shun.

Much has been said and written about the subjects of heaven and hell. Martin Luther stated, "I would not give one moment of Heaven for all the joy and riches of the world, even if it lasted for thousands of years."[21] Billy Sunday stated, "Better limp all the way to Heaven than not get there at all."[22] Alighieri Dante describes Hell as follows, "Here sighs, plaints, and voices of the deepest woe resounded through the starless sky. Strange languages, horrid cries, accents of grief and wrath, voices deep and hoarse, with hands clenched in despair, made a commotion which whirled forever through that air of everlasting gloom, even as sand when whirlwinds sweep the ground."[23] Numerous scriptures throughout the Bible corroborate the existence of Heaven and Hell. My friend, live your life in light of the eternal.

35

Serve The Lord

The story of Jesus raising Lazarus from the dead is of particular interest to me because of certain events that took place in the life of Lazarus after he was raised from the dead. I'll get into further details on why I say this later in this chapter. By the way, this is a different Lazarus than the one in the preceding story.

Jesus was away from Bethany when he heard of Lazarus being sick. He purposely tarried there two days longer before he left to go to Bethany. Upon arriving in Bethany, he was informed that Lazarus had been in the tomb for four days. Jesus, in reality, already knew that Lazarus had died before he arrived.

He had already planned to raise Lazarus from the dead before coming back to Bethany. Martha and Mary greeted Him with tears and Jesus was led to the tomb. Jesus commanded that the stone be moved and then proceeded to call Lazarus out. Lazarus, bound hand and foot with wrappings, came out of the tomb. Lazarus had just been raised from the dead in accordance with what Jesus had planned to do.

I've heard it taught that the Pharisees and Sadducees believed the spirit of man hovers over a body for three days, but after four days the man's spirit leaves the body for good. No man comes back after being dead for four days. The body decays. This is why I believe Jesus tarried the extra time. He wanted all to know that Lazarus was raised through the power of God. There would be no mistake concerning the presence of God in this event.

Many became believers after beholding this event, and rightly so. This clearly was an act of a divine nature. However, have you ever pondered what happened to Lazarus after this event? The scriptures tell us that the chief priests took counsel that they might put Lazarus to death. (John 12:10). With that in mind, I was in Larnaca, Cyprus in 1982 when I visited the Church of St. Lazarus. Tradition tells us that things got hot for Lazarus after he was raised from the dead. The chief priests wanted to kill him for he was living proof of the power of God through Jesus. Thus, Lazarus departed the area and proclaimed the gospel in Cyprus where he eventually died his second death.

This is of keen interest to me. Lazarus, who had been beyond life's door, returned to life and became on fire for Jesus Christ as he started a ministry in Cyprus. He knew what the afterlife held and it significantly influenced him on how he lived this life. He lived it spreading the gospel of Jesus Christ. His priorities in this life were to promote the Lord and tell others where they would go if they believed in Him. Make no mistake, I'm sure he shared and related his testimony of what glorious things awaited those in Christ Jesus.

I believe Lazarus' priorities were in order. In light of what he experienced, and actions of his life after he returned from the dead, are our priorities in order? Lazarus would tell you, if he were here, that there is life after death. Let us take note of his experience and how he came back from the dead to spread the gospel and live for Jesus Christ. This is not pie in the sky but reality. Serve the Lord, and again I say, serve the Lord.

Conclusion

These simple lessons will help us to live better lives as we apply them, but the most important biblical lesson and decision in a man's life is that of salvation. If there is any doubt as to your salvation, then I urge you to consider the following scriptures.

"As it is written, there is none righteous, not even one." (Romans 3:10).

"For all have sinned and fall short of the glory of God." (Romans 3:23).

"For the wages of sin is death, but the free gift of God is eternal life in Christ Jesus our Lord." (Romans 6:23).

"For there is one God, and one mediator also between God and men, the man Christ Jesus." (I Timothy 2:5).

"That if you confess with your mouth Jesus as Lord, and believe in your heart that God raised Him from the dead, you shall be saved; for with the heart man believes, resulting in righteousness, and with the mouth he confesses, resulting in salvation." (Romans 10:9–10).

Now, a Sinner's Prayer to receive Jesus as Lord and Savior. Please repeat the following prayer and mean it from your heart.

"Dear Heavenly Father, I come to You in the name of the Lord Jesus Christ. I ask you to forgive me of all my sins. I accept Jesus as my Lord and Savior and believe in my heart that He died on the cross for my sins and that You raised Him from the dead for my justification. I now repent and confess Jesus as my Lord and Savior. I thank You for saving me and ask that You would help me in my Christian walk."

I strongly encourage you to read your Bible daily to get to know the Lord better, talk to God daily in prayer and find a church where the Bible is taught as the complete Word of God.

Footnotes

1. The Ryrie Study Bible. New American Standard Translation. Copyright 1976, 1978 by The Moody Bible Institute, Chicago, Illinois, page 1663.

2. Ibid, page 216.

3. Bartlett's Familiar Quotations, compiled by John Bartlett. Copyright 1980 by Little, Brown and Company, Inc., Boston, Massachusetts, page 661.

4. The Home Book of Quotations, compiled by Burton Stevenson. Copyright 1967 by Dodd, Mead & Company, Inc., New York, New York, page 1488.

5. The Yale Shakespeare, The Second Part of King Henry The Sixth, edited by Tucker Brooke. Copyright 1923 by Yale University Press, page 46.

6. Ibid, page 14.

7. Ibid, page 8.

8. Ibid, page 1567.

9. 12,000 Religious Quotations, edited and compiled by Frank S. Mead. Copyright 1965 by Judy D. Mead, Baker Book House, Grand Rapids, Michigan, page 176.

10. The Ryrie Study Bible. New American Standard Translation. Copyright 1976, 1978 by The Moody Bible Institute, Chicago, Illinois, page 371.

11. Ibid, page 34.

12. 12,000 Religious Quotations, edited and compiled by Frank S. Mead. Copyright 1965 by Judy D. Mead, Baker Book House, Grand Rapids, Michigan, page 409.

13. Ibid, page 409.

14. The Ryrie Study Bible. New American Standard Translation. Copyright 1976, 1978 by The Moody Bible Institute, Chicago, Illinois, page 1678.

15. Ibid, page 1678.

16. Ibid, page 35.

17. Ibid, page 1897.

18. Ibid, page 1900.

19. Webster's New World Dictionary of the American Language. Copyright 1970 by The World Publishing Company, New York, New York, page 864.

20. Halley's Bible Handbook, by Henry H. Halley. Copyright 1965 by Halley's Bible Handbook, Inc., Zondervan Publishing House, Grand Rapids, Michigan, page 336.

21. 12,000 Religious Quotations, edited and compiled by Frank S. Mead. Copyright 1965 by Judy D. Mead, Baker Book House, Grand Rapids, Michigan, page 217.

22. Ibid, page 219.

23. Ibid, page 222.

About The Author

Commander Michael H. Imhof, U.S. Navy (ret.), was born in Fort Bragg, North Carolina and raised in Blasdell, New York. He attended the State University College of New York at Buffalo, where he received a Bachelor of Science degree. He was commissioned in 1973. After completing Basic Underwater Demolition/SEAL training in Coronado, California, Commander Imhof was assigned to SEAL Team TWO, and subsequent Naval Special Warfare and other type commands.

Commander Imhof, possessing a Naval Special Warfare designator, has served throughout the world in numerous positions. Assignments include Platoon Commander, Training Officer, Operations Officer, Staff Officer, Executive Officer and Commanding Officer. He also earned a Master's Degree in Administration from George Washington University and served as an instructor at the U.S. Naval Academy. His awards include Defense Meritorious Service Medal; Meritorious Service Medal with two Gold Stars in lieu of second and third awards; Joint Service Commendation Medal; Navy Commendation Medal with Gold Star in lieu of second award; United Nations Medal; and other service awards.

A military officer of strong Christian convictions, Commander Imhof is ready and willing to share his faith with all. He is convinced that the Bible is the authoritative and uncompromising Word of God and gives thanks for the wonderful blessings of God in his life and the lives of his family. He is an active member in his local church.